My Little Angel

PAINTINGS BY

Sandra Kuck

HARVEST HOUSE PUBLISHERS

EUGENE, OREGON

My Little Angel

Text Copyright © 2005 by Harvest House Publishers
Eugene, Oregon 97402

ISBN-13: 978-0-7369-1362-1
ISBN-10: 0-7369-1362-9

Design and production by Garborg Design Works, Minneapolis, Minnesota

Harvest House Publishers has made every effort to trace the ownership of all poems and quotes. In the event of a question arising from the use of a poem or quote, we regret any error made and will be pleased to make the necessary correction in future editions of this book.

Unless otherwise indicated, all Scripture quotations are taken from the Holy Bible, New International Version®. NIV®. Copyright © 1973, 1978, 1984 by the International Bible Society. Used by permission of Zondervan. All rights reserved. Scriptures marked KJV are from the King James Version of the Bible.

Printed in Hong Kong
07 08 09 10 11 12 / NG / 10 9 8 7 6 5 4

Children are living jewels dropped

unsustained from heaven.

ROBERT POLLOK

Every child is born a genius.

R. BUCKMINSTER FULLER

GROWN MEN CAN LEARN FROM VERY
LITTLE CHILDREN FOR THE HEARTS
OF LITTLE CHILDREN ARE PURE.

BLACK ELK

*We must teach

our children to

dream with their

eyes open.*

There are only two lasting bequests
we can hope to give our children.
One is roots; the other, wings.

CARTER HODDING

HARRY EDWARDS

5

The Tea Party

I had a little tea party this afternoon at three.
   'Twas very small, three guests in all,
Just I, myself, and me.

Myself ate up the sandwiches,
   While I drank up the tea.
'Twas also I who ate the pie,
   And passed the cake to me.

AUTHOR UNKNOWN

A CHILD IS
A BEAM OF
SUNLIGHT...
WITH
POSSIBILITIES
OF VIRTUE
AND VICE—
BUT AS YET
UNSTAINED.

LYMAN ABBOTT

Angels can fly because they take themselves lightly....

G.K. CHESTERTON

If we were all like angels,
the world would be a heavenly place.

AUTHOR UNKNOWN

Where Did You Come From?

Where did you come from, Baby dear?
  Out of the everywhere into here.

Where did you get your eyes so blue?
  Out of the sky as I came through.

What makes the light in them sparkle and spin?
  Some of the starry spikes left in.

Where did you get that little tear?
  I found it waiting when I got here.

What makes your forehead so smooth and high?
  A soft hand stroked it as I went by.

What makes your cheek like a warm white rose?
  I saw something better than anyone knows.

Whence that three-corner'd smile of bliss?
  Three angels gave me at once a kiss.

Where did you get this pearly ear?
  God spoke, and it came out to hear.

Where did you get those arms and hands?
  Love made itself into bonds and bands.

Feet, whence did you come, you darling things?
  From the same box as the cherubs' wings.

Where did you get that dimple so cute,
  God touched my cheek as I came through.

How did they all come just to be you?
  God thought of me, and so I grew.

But how did you come to us, you dear?
  God thought of you, and so I am here.

GEORGE MACDONALD

Before you were conceived I wanted you, before you were born I loved you, before you were here an hour I would die for you, this is the miracle of love.

MAUREEN HAWKINS

PERHAPS CHILDREN'S INNOCENCE, WHEREVER IT COMES FROM, CONTRIBUTES TO THE FACT THAT THEY SEEM TO SEE ANGELS MORE OFTEN.

JOHN RONNER

Silently one by one, in the infinite meadows of heaven Blossomed the lovely stars, the forget-me-nots, of angels.

HENRY WADSWORTH LONGFELLOW

Make yourself familiar with the angels, and behold them frequently in spirit; for without being seen, they are present with you.

ST. FRANCIS DE SALES

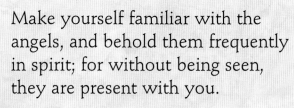

10

WHAT
FEELING IS
SO NICE AS
A CHILD'S
HAND IN
YOURS?
SO SMALL,
SO SOFT AND
WARM, LIKE
A KITTEN
HUDDLING
IN THE
SHELTER OF
YOUR CLASP.

MARJORIE
HOLMES

11

Angels remind us to look beyond our everyday circumstance or stress.

TIMOTHY JONES

GOD IS WATCHING, AND HIS ANGELS ARE INTERESTED SPECTATORS TOO.

BILLY GRAHAM

Father asked us what was God's noblest work. Anna said men, but I said babies. Men are often bad; babies never are.

LOUISA MAY ALCOTT

Children of the heav'nly Father
Safely in His bosom gather;
Nestling bird nor star in heaven
Such a refuge e'er was given.

Lo, their very hairs He numbers,
And no daily care encumbers
Them that share His ev'ry blessing
And His help in woes distressing.

KAROLINA SANDELL-BERG

13

Dear Lord,

Could You spare some guardian angels
To give us peace of mind
As our Children wander from us
And stretch the ties that bind?

You have Heavenly Legions, Father,
Could you send us just a few?
To guide our eager youngsters
As we give them, Lord, to You.

Oh Thank You, Thank You, Father,
And oh our glad hearts sing
We're certain that just now we heard
The swish of passing wings!

AUTHOR UNKNOWN

A BABY IS AN INESTIMABLE BLESSING AND BOTHER.

MARK TWAIN

If your baby is "beautiful and perfect, never cries or fusses, sleeps on schedule and burps on demand, an angel all the time," you're the grandma.

THERESA BLOOMINGDALE

We find delight in the beauty and happiness of children that makes the heart too big for the body.

RALPH WALDO EMERSON

A baby is God's opinion that the world should go on.

CARL SANDBURG

16

It is easier to build strong children
than to repair broken men.

FREDERICK DOUGLAS

I went forth to find an angel

And found this effort brought

That life is full of so much good

The touch that angels wrought.

JAMES JOSEPH HUESGEN

YOU CAN LEARN MANY THINGS FROM
CHILDREN. HOW MUCH PATIENCE
YOU HAVE, FOR INSTANCE.

FRANKLIN P. ADAMS

Our children are not going to be just "our children"— they are going to be other people's husbands and wives and the parents of our grandchildren.

MARY STEICHEN CALDERONE

A child reminds us that playtime is an essential part of our daily routine.

ANONYMOUS

A CHILD IS FED WITH MILK AND PRAISE.

MARY LAMB

I will give thanks to You, O lord, with all my heart, in the presence of the angels I will sing Your praise.

THE BOOK OF PSALMS

WHERE
CHILDREN
ARE,
THERE
IS THE
GOLDEN
AGE.

NOVALIS

If you raise your children to

feel that they can accomplish

any goal or task they decide

upon, you will have succeeded

as a parent and you will have

given your children the greatest

of all blessings.

BRIAN TRACY

Making the decision to have a child— it's momentous. It is to decide forever to have your heart go walking around outside your body.

ELIZABETH STONE

Children are the keys of paradise.

RICHARD HENRY STODDARD

My dishes went unwashed today,
I didn't make the bed,
I took his hand and followed
Where his eager footsteps led.
Oh yes, we went adventuring,
My little son and I . . .
Exploring all the great outdoors
Beneath the summer sky.

I Took His Hand and Followed

We waded in a crystal stream,
We wandered through a wood . . .
My kitchen wasn't swept today
But life was gay and good.
We found a cool, sun-dappled glade
And now my small son knows
How Mother Bunny hides her nest,
Where jack-in-the-pulpit grows.
We watched a robin feed her young,
We climbed a sunlit hill . . .
Saw cloud-sheep scamper through the sky,
We plucked a daffodil.

That my house was neglected,
That I didn't brush the stairs,
In twenty years, no one on earth
Will know, or even care.
But that I've helped my little boy
To noble manhood grow,
In twenty years, the whole wide world
May look and see and know.

AUTHOR UNKNOWN

24

A CHILD IS SOMEONE WHO PASSES THROUGH YOUR LIFE AND THEN DISAPPEARS INTO AN ADULT.

REGINALD HOLMES

Having a child is surely the most beautifully irrational act that two people in love can commit.

BILL COSBY

But especially he noted the children— first curiously, then eagerly, then lovingly. Ragged little ones rolled in the dust of the streets, playing with scraps and pebbles. Other children, gaily dressed, were propped upon cushions and fed with sugar-plums. Yet the children of the rich were not happier than those playing with the dust and pebbles, it seemed to Claus.

"Childhood is the time of man's greatest content," said Ak, following the youth's thoughts. "'Tis during these years of innocent pleasure that the little ones are most free from care."

FRANK BAUM
The Life and Adventures of Santa Claus

My Guardian Angel

Dear Angel ever at my side,
how lovely you must be—
To leave your home in heaven,
to guard a child like me.
When I'm far away from home,
or maybe hard at play—
I know you will protect me,
from harm along the way.
Your beautiful and shining face,
I see not, though you're near.
The sweetness of your lovely voice,
I cannot really hear.
When I pray, you're praying too,
Your prayer is just for me.
But,when I sleep you never do,
You're watching over me.

AUTHOR UNKNOWN

A HAPPY FAMILY
IS BUT AN
EARLIER HEAVEN.

SIR JOHN BOWRING

THE SWEETEST
ROAMER IS A
BOY'S YOUNG
HEART.

G.E. WOODBERRY

CHILDREN
AND
MOTHERS
NEVER
TRULY
PART—
BOUND
IN THE
BEATING
OF EACH
OTHER'S
HEART.

CHARLOTTE
GRAY

27

*How delicate
the skin,
how sweet the
breath of
children!*

EURIPIDES

28

Children—
the fruit of the seeds of all your finest hopes.

GLORIA GAITHER

FOR HE SHALL
GIVE HIS
ANGELS CHARGE
OVER THEE TO
KEEP THEE IN
ALL THY WAYS.

THE BOOK OF
PSALMS (KJV)

He ruffles through his hymn book,

He fumbles with his tie,

He laces up his oxfords,

He overworks a sigh;

He goes through all his pockets,

Engrossed in deep research;

There's no one quite so busy

As a little boy in church.

THELMA IRELAND

CHILDHOOD IS THE WORLD OF MIRACLE
AND WONDER: AS IF CREATION ROSE,
BATHED IN LIGHT, OUT OF THE DARKNESS,
UTTERLY NEW AND FRESH AND ASTONISHING.

EUGENE IONESCO

A Little Girl's Heart

A little girl's heart must be wide and deep,
To hold all the things that she likes to keep;
A curly-haired doll that holds out its hands
And walks and talks when occasion demands.
A bright colored bow, her favorite book,
A little toy stove that really will cook;
A gay, cheery song, to sing when she's glad,
A corner to hide in (when she's been bad).
There is plenty of room for the girl next door
And the blue silk dress in the downtown store;
A soft fluffy kitten with playful charms
And a welcome spot in her mother's arms.

AUTHOR UNKNOWN

Let the little children come to me, and do not hinder them, for the kingdom of heaven belongs to such as these.

THE BOOK OF
MATTHEW

31

Blessed be the childhood,

which brings down something of heaven

into the midst of our rough earthliness.

HENRI FREDERIC AMIEL